Bedtime Prayers

Nadeen Bucknor

Bedtime Prayers

Book Illustrator: Isha Trotman
Contributor: Jayson Bucknor

Copyright@ 2017 by Nadeen Brown, USA
All rights reserved
ISBN-978-0-9977282-4-8
Prints in the United States of America

Dedication...

To all my precious students

Table of Content

1. Prayer of Thanksgiving
2. Prayer of Protection
3. Prayer About God's Love
4. Prayer For Fear
5. Prayer For Rejection
6. Prayer For Nightmare
7. Prayer For Depression
8. Prayer About My Identity
9. Prayer For Healing
10. Prayer For Wisdom
11. Prayer For Family
12. Prayer For Friends
13. Salvation Prayer

Prayer of Thanksgiving

Dear God,
Thank you for keeping me throughout this day.

I will always give God thanks!

Prayer of Protection

Powerful God,

Thank you for protecting me from every hurt, harm and danger.

I am so grateful to You for keeping me safe!

God protects me from all danger!

Prayer of God's Love

Dear God,

I know You love me greatly!

You give me parents that love me; a place to live; a bed to sleep in; food to eat and lots of wonderful presents, too many to count!

Prayer For Fear

Dear kind and loving God,
Let Your perfect love remove every fear right now, from my life!
Because the love of God covers me, I am no longer afraid.
Thank you for Your love, which makes me as bold as a lion in Jesus Name I pray! Amen!

God loves me! So I do not fear!

Prayer For Rejection

I decree and declare that I am created, loved and accepted by God!

I am a significant member in the Family of God! And no one, nor any power of darkness can change that!

Accepted by God...never rejected!

Prayer For Nightmare

Every evil power that brings bad thoughts and dreams to torment me during the night,
Be removed by the Fire of God!
And be replaced with good thoughts and dreams!

No nightmares...good dreams

Prayer For Depression

In the Name of Jesus, I bind and remove every power of sadness, oppression and depression that has been tormenting my life!

Let the fire of God permanently destroy all evil plans set in motion, to take away my peace.

Instead of sadness, let the joy of the Lord fill my soul and life forever!

Depression be gone!

Prayer About Identity

Almighty God, You created me in your perfect image! I reject, uproot and cast out everything and anything that would create a false identity in me. I lose myself from every faulty body image in my mind and I break free from every peer pressure that opposes who God said I am. Thank you Lord, for causing me to walk in my true God given identity! In Jesus Name I pray!

My identity is perfect in Christ!

Prayer For Healing

Almighty God,

You said, healing belongs to Your children!

So, I believe You Lord that I am healed in my body, soul and spirit in Jesus precious Name I pray! Amen!

I am healed!

24

Prayer For Wisdom

Heavenly Father,

All good things come from You, the only wise God! Let me know Your Will for my life in every situation, as I grow in wisdom and spiritual understanding! In Jesus Name I pray! Amen

I have the wisdom of God!

Prayer For Family

Powerful God,

Release Your strength over every dark force that has been attacking the lives of my family members and I.
Let Your power break every chain that has kept us in bondage!
In the power of Jesus Name I pray! Amen!

My family is free from every chain!

Prayer For Friends

Lord you mean so much to me!
I thank you that you are a friend who sticks close to me and stands up for me, especially when I am too small to defend myself!

God is a friend...who defends me!

Prayer About Salvation

Dear Jesus,
I invite You into my heart and life today,
Be my Lord and Savior.
Please forgive me,
Cleanse me of all my sins
And let my life be filled with more of you each day!

Today is the day of salvation...Lord I give you my heart.

Amen!

Author

Nadeen Bucknor is the author of several children and adult books. She is a certified K-12 teacher of Biology and General Science in New Jersey and the founder of Blaze Academy, a Christian school that serves children from pre-K to secondary school age. Nadeen was also a Sunday school teacher for many years and loves to teach about prayer.

Contact Information

Email: nadeenbrown.nb@gmail.com

Twitter: NadeenBrown@nadeen_brown